21 PRAYERS OF THANKSGIVING

Transform Your Prayer Life by Giving Thanks

Rachel Larkin

21 Prayers of Thanksgiving:
Transform Your Prayer Life by Giving Thanks

© 2019 Rachel Larkin

ISBN 978-0-473-45261-2

All rights reserved. No part of this publication may be reproduced, stored in a retrieval system, or transmitted by any means- electronic, mechanical, photographic (photocopying), recording, or otherwise - without prior permission in writing from the author, unless it is for the furtherance of the Gospel of salvation and given away free of charge. Although every precaution has been taken to verify the accuracy of the information contained herein, the author and publisher assume no responsibility for any errors or omissions. No liability is assumed for damages that may result from the use of information contained within.

Unless otherwise indicated, all Scripture quotations are taken from the Holy Bible, New Living Translation, copyright ©1996, 2004, 2007, 2013, 2015 by Tyndale House Foundation. Used by permission of Tyndale House Publishers, Inc., Carol Stream, Illinois 60188. All rights reserved.

CONTENTS

How To Use This Book 5
10 Ways Thankfulness Transforms Our Prayers 7
1. Your Children 11
2. Your Teenagers 13
3. Your Spouse 15
4. Your Church 19
5. Your Home 21
6. Your Friends 23
7. Your Health 25
8. Your Protection 27
9. Your Work 29
10. Your Weakness 31
11. Your Time 33
12. Your Future 35
13. God's Provision 37
14. God's Grace 39
15. God's Love 41
16. God's Joy 43
17. God's Forgiveness 45
18. God's Word 47
19. God's Creation 49
20. Jesus' Prayer 51
21. Jesus' Name 53
Other Books By Rachel Larkin 55
Free Ebook 57
About The Author 59

HOW TO USE THIS BOOK

Biblical Thanksgiving is an everyday spiritual tool. But sometimes we let our ordinary daily lives overwhelm us and we forget to include thanksgiving in our prayers.

This book will provide 21 thanksgiving prayer ideas that will help you think in a thanksgiving way towards God. It takes scripture on 21 areas and draws out the goodness related to giving thanks. Then you can join in the prayer and give your own thanks to your wonderful Father God.

10 WAYS THANKFULNESS TRANSFORMS OUR PRAYERS

"It is a good thing to give thanks unto the Lord."
Psalm 92:1

We all want good things in our life and regularly giving thanks to God is a good thing. The Hebrew word for good in Psalm 92:1 is tov. It means something pleasant and agreeable to the senses. Something that brings happiness, welfare, and favor. Something that functions properly is good and in turn this makes us glad.

Giving thanks transforms our life and surroundings but it also can transform our prayers. Praying to God is just talking and listening to Him. It is like breathing – a regular activity that we often take for granted but it is vital for staying alive. When we wrap thanksgiving around our prayers something powerful is released and God is given the space to work in our lives and prayers.

1. Giving Thanks Opens Our Eyes to the Unseen

It's hard to see the spiritual in the midst of the natural. Our busyness with life's details seem to take over the spiritual. Giving thanks opens our eyes to see behind the scenes of life, to see the story that God is weaving through our daily moments – the untold story.

"So, we fix our eyes not on what is seen, but on what is unseen. For what is seen is temporary, but what is unseen is eternal."
2 Corinthians 4:18

2. Giving Thanks Shifts Our Focus onto Jesus

"[looking away from all that will distract us and] focusing our eyes on Jesus, who is the Author and Perfecter of faith…"
Hebrews 12:2a AMP

There are so many things in this life that distract us from Jesus and the growing of our faith. Giving thanks is a trigger that once activated regularly aligns our thoughts onto Jesus and all that He has accomplished for us. One prayer of thanksgiving today can move your focus from earthly things to heavenly things.

3. Thanksgiving is a Reminder of His Goodness and Love

"Praise the Lord! Oh, give thanks to the Lord, for he is good, for his steadfast love endures forever! Psalm 106:1

Believing, deep down, in the truth that God is love, and He is good, builds our faith and banishes fear. Can you imagine living fear free? A place of freedom, where we come boldly into God's throne room to lay our requests and fears at His feet, knowing that He loves us deeply. Remembering all the wonderful blessings in our life on a regular basis brings us into a spacious, open place of freedom.

4. Thanksgiving Draws us into His Presence

"Surely the righteous shall give thanks to your name; the upright shall dwell in your presence." Psalm 140:13

As we praise and give thanks to our Father, we are drawn into His very presence. His presence gives us rest (Exodus 33:14), it fulfills promises (Genesis 28:15), it fills us with joy and the knowledge of the path of life (Psalm 16:11), fear is gone and comfort reigns (Psalm 23:4), we are hidden from the plots of men (Psalm 31:20), mountains melt like wax (Psalm 97:5) and we are surrounded by His love (1 John 4:16). His presence is the place to listen and talk to God.

5. Thanksgiving is the key that unlocks our conversations with God

"Enter his gates with thanksgiving; go into his courts with praise. Give thanks to him and praise his name." Psalm 100:4

Starting our prayers thanking God is not just following a set pattern, it's the key that unlocks the secret to effective prayer. Thanksgiving makes God look glorious – "The one who offers thanksgiving as his sacrifice glorifies me" Psalm 50:23.

6. Giving Thanks Pleases God

"In everything give thanks. For this is God's will (desire) for you in Christ Jesus." 1 Thessalonians 5:18

What is the will of God? Most Believers will confess their confusion about the will of God. But 1 Thessalonians 5:18 is very clear – when we give thanks in everything then we are doing exactly what God desires. Since giving thanks to God in everything touches His heart – let's wrap our prayers, like a present, in thanksgiving.

7. Being Thankful Brings Clarity in Decisions

A couple of years ago, we were going through a hard time with health issues, job loss, decisions on where to live – a whole host of overwhelming problems. We didn't know how to solve them or what the next step would be. I remember feeling very close to giving up, so I went for a walk and started talking to God –God, I am so confused, what is our next step?

He clearly spoke to me – Child, your next step is always to give thanks, in everything.

8. Thanking God Keeps Us Hopeful

"But I will hope continually and will praise you yet more and more."
Psalm 71:14 ESV

There is a praise – hope cycle that takes place after acts of thanksgiving. The more we praise and thank Him the more we are filled with hope. The more hopeful we are in our God, the more our prayers are filled with thanksgiving. If we want hope and not discouragement – spend time thanking God.

9. Thanking God Banishes Fear and Doubt

As we come to the altar, knowing that God is the one in control, this infuses boldness into our hearts and prayers. Focusing on what He has done in the past and what He can perform in the future banishes doubt and fear – the two enemies of our prayers.

10. Miracles Follow Thanksgiving

There is room for the miraculous after thanksgiving. Jesus took a young boy's tiny lunch of fish and bread, gave thanks to God, and distributed more than enough to feed 5,000 men, with 12 baskets of leftovers. If a miracle is needed – start and continue to thank God – then watch for God to work.

YOUR CHILDREN

"I will teach all your children, and they will enjoy great peace."
Isaiah 54:13

"Children are a gift from the Lord they are a reward from Him."
Psalm 127:3

Our children are a blessing straight from God Himself. Sometimes in the midst of daily parenting we can become overwhelmed and forget the gift that they are.

How often do we complain about the shortcomings of our sons and daughters? How often do we thank God for the human gifts that He has given to us?

Children have a wonderful capacity to enjoy each moment as it comes without worrying about the details of life like adults do. They remind us to value each moment and to live in the present.

They display the concept of play which as adults we tend to lose as soon as we take on responsibilities of keeping a house and providing for our families. It's good to take time out and reconnect with the joy of play through our children.

Kids can say the darnedest things - isn't that true? They have been known to say the truth even when that may not be the most socially acceptable thing to say. Let's treasure their truth speaking values.

Children seem to be always full of questions. Sometimes this can be tiring - "but why?" is a question that is commonly repeated. But curiosity is a good thing! Let's be thankful for their inquiring minds.

My sons have taught me to think outside my myself. They have given me the opportunity to love another human being wholeheartedly. There is no time or space to be selfish when there are little ones around.

What a privilege we have as parents to pass on our values, beliefs, opinions, thoughts, and dreams to our kids. This 'passing down' is a valuable ministry that sometimes gets devalued over time. What an opportunity! It's a 24-hour mission from God. Our encouraging words, daily smiles and bear hugs are their soul food.

Let's thank God for our children.

Thanksgiving Prayer

Thank you, God, for my children. Thank you that you have promised to teach my children. Thank you for your promise that they will enjoy great peace because you are our Father (Isaiah 54:13)

Sometimes Lord, parenting is so daunting and tiring but I praise you for giving them to me. Thank you that my children are a reward and gift from you. Please help me today to see them as precious gifts straight from your hand (Psalm 127:3). Thank you that each child is special, unique, and crafted by you. I praise you that they are wonderfully created (Psalm 139). Thank you that you have a plan specially designed for each one of my children (Jeremiah 29:11). Thank you Lord that as I direct my children onto the right path for their lives that when they are older they will not leave it (Proverbs 22:6). I thank you for matching my unique children to me. Not one child is a mistake in your eyes. They are precious in your sight and I thank you for them. In the name of Jesus, amen.

YOUR TEENAGERS

"Direct your children onto the right path, and when they are older, they will not leave it." Proverbs 22:6

"Young people, it's wonderful to be young! Enjoy every minute of it. Do everything you want to do; take it all in. But remember that you must give an account to God for everything you do." Ecclesiastes 11:9

Ah, teenagers - how do they grow so fast? One minute they are needing your help to tie up their shoes and ride their bike, the next they are asking to borrow the car. Teenagers are amazing. At this stage in their live, some of our parenting efforts start to pay dividends. But on the other side, some parenting mistakes start to come home to roost.

Our society puts teenagers down. I have not read or heard of many thankful parents of teenagers - which is very disheartening. This is the time where you know you love them fiercely but some of you wonder whether you like your teenagers. Let's stop the trend of putting teenagers down. Let's start a revolution of being thankful for your teenagers.

This revolution starts by seeking to understand our teenagers' hearts. Sometimes the outside actions and words of our teenager camouflage their deep fears for the future. Ask God to help you see past their outside exterior and right into their hearts. They still need your encouragement and praise. They still need to know that you value them as a person.

Talk well of your teen to people. Don't for one minute put your teen down in conversation. This is basic respectful behavior. Fight for the good name of teenagers. Love your teens with the same love that you had for them as children.

Be thankful for their fun and laughter. Spend time at the dinner table conversing in their world - take on their peculiar language, have fun with it.

I am so amazed at how inventive teens can be. If given the chance they can come up with creative solutions to the predicaments, they find themselves in. Be available and approachable for those teaching times - they will come, most probably late at night when they decide it is time to talk.

Catch their enthusiasm. Marvel at their energy. Allow them time to sleep. Don't become too serious. Have fun along with them. Be open to their dreams.

Teenagers help us as parents to rely on God. It's time to give them over to God for His protection. They are starting to move out from under your guidance and your physical home. Be thankful for this opportunity to personally grow in your trust and reliance on God for your growing young adults.

Thanksgiving Prayer

Thank you, Father, for my teenagers. They are still a gift from your hand. You have matched them perfectly to our family. Thank you for their growth, thank you for the opportunity of teaching them while they were young. Even though I am not a perfect parent, I thank you that you are crafting them into your image. I thank you for their energy, their love for everything new and their funny stories. Please help me to understand my teens heart. I thank you for working in their hearts. I pray that they will grow in the knowledge of Jesus. I pray that they will know that you love them lavishly. I give my teen over to you, for your protection and care. Thank you for the opportunity to love _____ (insert your teens name). I pray this in the name of Jesus, amen.

YOUR SPOUSE

"I want them to be encouraged and knit together by strong ties of love."
Colossians 2:2a

"Then the Lord God said, "It is not good for the man to be alone. I will make a helper who is just right for him." Genesis 2:18

"A person standing alone can be attacked and defeated, but two can stand back-to-back and conquer. Three are even better, for a triple-braided cord is not easily broken." Ecclesiastes 4:12

It is not often that I hear prayers of thanksgiving for spouses. I hear a lot of prayers for change and complaints about husbands and wives, but rarely do I hear prayers of thanks. None of us are perfect, not one. Both partners come into a marriage with baggage, unresolved triggers, and issues. But if God is invited as the third party, something beautiful can happen. It only takes one of the two partners to connect with God in a personal relationship to have a tremendous effect on the marriage.

Paul's desire for the Colossians, to be knitted together by strong ties of love, has been my top marriage prayer. The times I most often whisper this prayer to God is during times of disagreement. God has never disappointed me. I have found a genuine love grow between us like rope being wrapped around an object creating a strong bond.

Your life partner was chosen and handpicked by God. I strongly believe that He is the ultimate matchmaker. If you are waiting to meet your future life partner - don't become anxious - keep trusting, keep on carrying out God's plan for your life and start thanking God for the one that He has chosen. God's timing is perfect. Thanksgiving is our ultimate tool for times of waiting. Waiting for a partner and waiting for a partner to change and give their hearts to God.

Your partner may be completely different to you - celebrate the differences instead of complaining about them. There is a reason God matched you together. Thank God for his spontaneity while you are organized. Thank God for her extrovert nature that sometimes is annoying. Thank God for his thriftiness and hardworking attitude. There is always something to thank God for in your partner.

Challenge yourself - think of one thing about your partner that you can thank God for each day this week. If this seems hard to you - ask God to show you what you can be thankful for. Ask God to open your eyes to see what He sees in your partner. Once you start looking and observing, the thanksgiving will flow. Take it a step further and verbalize thanks to your partner. Don't allow the many years of your marriage to dull your gratitude for who God has bought into your life. Thanksgiving is the tool that will breathe life and love into any relationship, especially the love relationship between a man and a woman.

Thanksgiving Prayer

Thank you, God, for handpicking my partner for me. Thank you for knitting us together with strong ties of love today. Please help me to remember you in times of disagreement. Thank you, Father, that you value my marriage relationship and want to strengthen it daily. Thank you Lord that I am not alone, that you have chosen someone to share my joys, sorrows, and life with. Thank you for being in our relationship as part of a triple-braided cord that is not easily broken. Thank you for my partners personality, skills, and love for me. Help us to daily grow together with You as the center. In the name of Jesus, amen.

YOUR CHURCH

"The human body has many parts, but the many parts make up one whole body. So, it is with the body of Christ… This makes for harmony among the members, so that all the members care for each other. If one part suffers, all the parts suffer with it, and if one part is honored, all the parts are glad. All of you together are Christ's body, and each of you is a part of it." 1 Corinthians 12:12,25-27

"Together, we are his house, built on the foundation of the apostles and the prophets. And the cornerstone is Christ Jesus himself. We are carefully joined together in him, becoming a holy temple for the Lord. Through him you Gentiles are also being made part of this dwelling where God lives by his Spirit." Ephesians 2:20-22

"This is the church of the living God, which is the pillar and foundation of the truth." 1 Timothy 3:15

"A spiritual gift is given to each of us, so we can help each other." 1 Corinthians 12:7

"And let the peace that comes from Christ rule in your hearts. For as members of one body you are called to live in peace. And always be thankful." Colossians 3:15

Church, the body of Christ, is a good thing created and indwelt by God. Church is not a building but a body of people around the earth in whom the Spirit dwells inside. The church is not man made so no one can boast. Christ, the cornerstone, carefully joins each one of us together - so that we can become a holy temple for the Lord.

It's alive, it's active, it's a place where there is harmony and caring. Suffering isn't frowned upon - it's surrounded with care. Success isn't scorned - it's honored, and the praise goes back to Jesus. It's the very backbone of truth. Spiritual gifts are given. Help is abundant. Peace reigns in the hearts. It all returns to God in thanks.

✷ Pray and ask God to direct you to your place in His body. God has a place where you can be built up in your faith and be a blessing to others. A place where you will find help, teaching, care, peace, and love. A place where you can serve, give, worship and support others. Pray for your church body and leaders.

Thanksgiving Prayer

Oh, thank you Lord for creating a body of believers, indwelt with your Spirit. Thank you for the truth that is in your church. It's You that carefully joins each one of us together as a church. Please help me to find my place to be in your church. Thank you that Jesus is the center, the cornerstone of Your people. Praise you for the differences in my church - differences in culture, ethnicity, skills, gifting, and personalities. I pray that You will knit us together in love and peace. Help us to support each other. Help us to bring You all the praise and glory. In the name of Jesus, amen.

YOUR HOME

"Now all glory to God, who is able, through his mighty power at work within us, to accomplish infinitely more than we might ask or think."
Ephesians 3:20

"Then Lord God planted a garden in Eden in the east, and there he placed the man he had made." Genesis 2:8

"He led them straight to safety, to a city where they could live."
Psalm 107:7

"My people will live in safety, quietly at home. They will be at rest."
Isaiah 32:18

"A house is built by wisdom and becomes strong through good sense. Through knowledge its rooms are filled with all sorts of precious riches and valuables." Proverbs 24:3-4

    Let's start by dwelling on the *bigness* of our God. Praise God, He can provide a home for you and your family. In fact, He can accomplish infinitely more than we can even imagine! He created all the necessary materials that goes into making a home. He owns the cattle on a thousand hills. Nothing is impossible for Him. The question is not whether He is *able* but is He *willing* to provide a home? Yes, I believe He is able *and* willing to provide shelter for His sons and daughters just like any good earthly father would want to.

He gave a specially designed home for Adam to live - the garden of Eden. God purposefully designed Adam's place. Then he placed Adam there. The Word tells us that He provides and cares for even the tiniest bird. He provides them with materials to create their nests. He even provides the trees for the nests. If God cares that much for the birds - how much more does He care for us - His children.

God has a home prepared for you, here on earth and in heaven. As He led the Israelites to the promised land - a place that God had planned for them to live - He can lead you and your family to a city where you can live.

God's desire is for His people to live in safety and rest - even if there is turmoil in your neighborhood - there can be rest and safety within. Allow God to build your home with the materials of wisdom and understanding. Invite Jesus to fill your rooms with the knowledge of Him - which is more precious than costly furnishings.

Thanksgiving Prayer

Father God, you are a big God, you can provide shelter and a home for our family. I thank you for your provision. I thank you that you have a place picked out for us to live just as you did for Adam and the Israelites. Father, lead us to our place. Just as you lead the birds of the air to the materials they need to build their nests, I thank you that you desire to lead us in how to build our homes. Thank you for building our home by your wisdom not our own. Thanks for making our homes strong by your understanding and good sense. Thank you for filling our rooms with precious treasures through knowledge of Jesus. In the name of Jesus, I pray, amen.

YOUR FRIENDS

"There are "friends" who destroy each other, but a real friend sticks closer than a brother." Proverbs 18:24

"Walk with the wise and become wise; associate with fools and get in trouble." Proverbs 13:20

"An open rebuke is better than hidden love! Wounds from a sincere friend are better than many kisses from an enemy." Proverbs 27:5-6

"Two people are better off than one, for they can help each other succeed. If one person falls, the other can reach out and help. But someone who falls alone is in real trouble." Ecclesiastes 4:9-10

"As iron sharpens iron, so a friend sharpens a friend." Proverbs 27:17

"The godly give good advice to their friends; the wicked lead them astray." Proverbs 12:26

"There is no greater love than to lay down one's life for one's friends. You are my friends if you do what I command." John 15:13-14

They say that you can choose your friends, but you are stuck with your family. What type of friends have you chosen? What type of friend are you? Have you ever taken the time to thank God for your friends? I remember a time when I was a young girl, around 9 or 10, and my one prayer request was for a good friend. They seemed to be in short supply. My mother used to say - *"To have a good friend you must be a good friend."*

What is a good friend? A person who sticks by you and is not out to pull you down. A wise person who is not interested in seeking out trouble. A person who is not afraid to speak the truth out of love. A person who doesn't tell you want you want to hear but speaks with honesty for your good. A person who wants to see their friend succeed. When their friend falls, they are right there to help them back up. A person who gives advice for good not evil. A person who keeps you sharp, who helps question your motives and encourages you to stay on the right path.

The amazing truth on friendship is in John 15 where Jesus declares His friendship with anyone who is willing to follow Him. If you had no other earthly friends - Jesus can be your constant companion and friend - He is all you really need.

Thanksgiving Prayer

Thank you, Father, for providing me with good friends. Help me to appreciate them and to be a good friend back. Show me where I am failing in my friendships. Thank you for the times when my friends pull me up on my behavior and thinking. Thank you for friends who sharpen me like iron sharpens iron, even though it is uncomfortable at the time. I thank you for their influence in my life. Thank you, Jesus, for being my ultimate friend, for giving the supreme sacrifice, your life, for me. Thank you that I am no longer a slave but a friend of God. In the name of Jesus, amen.

YOUR HEALTH

"He sent his word and healed them, snatching them from the door of death. Let them praise the Lord for his great love and for the wonderful things he has done for them. Let them offer sacrifices of thanksgiving and sing joyfully about his glorious acts." Psalm 107:20-22

"He personally carried our sins in his body on the cross so that we can be dead to sin and live for what is right. By his wounds you are healed."
1 Peter 2:24

"A cheerful heart is good medicine, but a broken spirit saps a person's strength." Proverbs 17:22

"I will reward them with a long life and give them my salvation"
Psalm 91:16

Giving thanks for healing when we are well is easy isn't it? But often, when we are well we take our health for granted and forget to thank God for his healing. God has created an amazing self-healing body that seems to cope even when we give it hordes of junk food, little rest, and sometimes enormous stress. Take time out to thank God daily for the health of yourself and your family. An easy way to remember is to include it when you pray over your food.

Now, giving thanks while we are sick can be hard - it takes faith, doesn't it? It takes immersing yourself in God's Word, discovering what He says about sickness and health. His Word says that He is one who heals us, He sends His word for healing and He is the rewarder of long life.

Thanksgiving has a therapeutic effect on the mind and body. The Word tells us that a cheerful heart (which comes from a thankful attitude) is medicine for our body. It has been proven that laughter decreases the levels of cortisol, which are stress hormones in our body. Cortisol acts by constricting our blood vessels while good endorphins are released when we laugh. It's interesting that Psalm 107 bundles healing with thanksgiving.

There are many issues related to healing, the "whys" and "how's" and "when will I be healed" questions are hard to answer. But we know that God loves us. We know that He has a good plan for us. We know that whatever happens God will bring good out of it all. Trust Him and be thankful while you wait.

Thanksgiving Prayer

Father God, thank you for creating me. You know everything about me. You know when and where I hurt. You know the cells of my body - the good ones and the bad ones. Father I thank you for your healing Word. I pray that you will open my eyes to see, understand and trust in your healing words today. I praise you for your great love. I thank you for the wonderful things that you have done for me. Thank you for Jesus who bore wounds in his body so that I would be healed in mine. Please help me foster a cheerful heart today. Keep my spirit, my inner man strong. Thank you Lord for your healing power, I trust and wait for you. In the name of Jesus, amen.

YOUR PROTECTION

"You have always put a wall of protection around him and his home and his property." Job 1:10

"The Lord is my rock, my fortress, and my savior; my God is my rock, in whom I find protection. He is my shield, the power that saves me, and my place of safety." Psalm 18:2

"He will cover you with his feathers. He will shelter you with his wings. His faithful promises are your armor and protection." Psalm 91:4

"The Lord will be our Mighty One. He will be like a wide river of protection that no enemy can cross, that no enemy ship can sail upon." Isaiah 33:21

"But the Lord is faithful, he will strengthen you and guard (protect) you from the evil one." 2 Thessalonians 3:3

Oh, the Word is rich with statements on the protection of God. "Protection" is an old Latin word which literally means, *to cover in front*. The Word describes God's protection as a wall or hedge in the book of Job. The Hebrew word for hedge is *sook,* which means to entwine by shutting in like growing a hedge of thorns. In modern day vocabulary - "Hedging in" is building a tall wall or fence that is impenetrable. This hedge was a tangible wall of protection around Job, his home, family, and his property. The enemy knew it was there and had no way for breaking through without God's permission.

In the Psalms, His protection is illustrated as a place of refuge like a fortress or the clef of a rock. Some secret closed off area where you can live safely and securely. A refuge inside a mountain - immovable.

I love the picture of Psalm 91 with God covering us with his feathers - a wing shelter. A bird covers her young with her own wings, putting their own bodies between them and danger. They may receive the wounds that were meant for their young ones. Isn't that what Jesus has done? - by His wounds we are healed. Jesus put His own body on the line for us - the ultimate protection.

The image of armor and shields speak of protection. Psalm 91 talks about God's promises as our armor and shield. Knowing and believing on the promises of God keeps our minds in peace and protects our hearts from turmoil.

What are we protected from? Evil, the enemy, temptation that is too much to handle, sin, worry, the past, a hopeless future. The storms still come but we can survive them because our life is in His hands.

Thanksgiving Prayer

Thank you, Father, for being my protection like a hedge or wall surrounding my life and everyone dear to me. Thank you for your promises that are true and faithful - they are a shield covering me. You are my rock, my fortress, my God in who I trust. Thank you for your loving arms surrounding me like eagle's wings. Thank you for protecting me from evil and schemes of the enemy. Even though I may go through a storm today, I know that you will bring me through - my life is in your hands. Praise you Jesus. Amen.

YOUR WORK

"And may the Lord our God show us his approval and make our efforts successful. Yes, make our efforts successful." Psalm 90:17

"A hard worker has plenty of food, but a person who chases fantasies has no sense." Proverbs 12:11

"Work brings profit, but mere talk leads to poverty!" Proverbs 14:23

"Commit your actions to the Lord, and your plans will succeed." Proverbs 16:3

"For I can do everything through Christ who gives me strength." Philippians 4:13

"So, whether you eat or drink, or whatever you do, do it all for the glory of God." 1 Corinthians 10:31

Our work-life is very important to God. He wants to be an integral part of every area of our lives. It's so easy to turn our spiritual eyes and ears off when we enter our workplaces. What if we soak our work, our efforts, our ambitions in prayer and thanksgiving? What difference would it make?

Thank God for His favor and approval on your work. Ask Him to make your efforts successful. Another version of Psalm 90:17 says "Let the favor of the Lord our God be upon us; And confirm for us the work of our hands Yes. Confirm the work of our hands." (NASB) The Hebrew word for *confirm* is *kuwn;* it means to be firm, established, set up and enduring.

Isn't that what we all want? For our work to influence the world - something enduring.

Bring your work to the Lord with open hands. Offer it up to Him as worship. Ask yourself - Am I chasing fantasies, worthless things or am I working in the right area? Am I just all talk in my work and nothing gets done? Do I honestly commit my work and plans to the Lord or do I seek His seal of approval after I have made the decisions?

The Hebrew word for *commit* in Proverbs 16:3 is *galal* which is an image of a giant bolder being rolled away or a wave of water rolling in to shore. Take time out today, to roll your actions, work and plans onto the Lord. You may feel a hesitancy to do that - *what if God wants me to change what I am doing? What if He wants me to do something that is too hard?* Do we truly trust in God, the creator of heaven and earth? Wouldn't His ideas be far better than our own? Doesn't He promise us strength through Christ to carry out His plans?

Our work is our worship. So, whatever you do for your work, do it for the glory of God.

Thanksgiving Prayer

Thank you, God, that you are interested in every area of my life - not just my church and family life but also my work life. Thank you for your favor and approval on my work. If there is any part of my work that is not under your favor and approval, please reveal it to me today. I ask that you confirm the work of my hands. Thank you for the promise of provision for hard work. I commit and roll my work and plans onto you, Lord. I praise your name for the strength that is mine today through Christ. I want my work to be worship and bring you glory, Lord. In the name of Jesus, amen.

YOUR WEAKNESS

"Have compassion on me, O Lord, for I am weak." Psalm 6:2

"He gives power to the weak and strength to the powerless." Isaiah 40:29

"If I must boast, I would rather boast about the things that show how weak I am." 2 Corinthians 11:30

"When I am weak then I am strong." 2 Corinthians 12:10b

"My health may fail, and my spirit may grow weak, but God remains the strength of my heart; he is mine forever." Psalm 73:26

Every one of us has weaknesses. It could be your health. You might be bed ridden right now and thinking, *how can God use me?* You could have a disability that stops you from being part of something. You might be too young or too old, too big, or too small. Maybe you are too shy and find it difficult in social situations. Your weakness could be a temptation that just never seems to stop taunting you - comfort eating, addictions, spending money unwisely, greed, jealousy, keeping grudges. Take comfort, all the "greats" of the Bible had weaknesses too.

King David should have been out fighting with his army, but we find him at home peering out his window into his neighbor's house. Desire for what was not his took a hold of his heart. David didn't turn to God immediately but entertained that desire. It led down a path of adultery, lies, deception and murder. But He didn't stay there, he returned to God and was restored and became the man after God's own heart.

Peter had great self-confidence and even boasted that he would never turn his back on Jesus. But in the middle of the toughest night of his life, he did the very thing that he was so sure he would never do - he denied the Master. Not once. But three times. He didn't stay full of fear for long. Instead of fear he become filled with the Spirit and went on to speaking out to a crowd of over 2,000 people about Jesus.

A new mindset is needed when it comes to our failures and weaknesses. Paul made an amazing discovery about his weaknesses - God was made bigger! Being weak was a good thing, it provides the perfect environment for us to move out of the way and let God show up. Paul described our weaknesses as a basic earthen vessel - nothing special about it. The flaws and imperfections are many. But there is treasure inside. The power of the Holy Spirit working in and through us. Father God has a soft spot for the weak. Jesus came to seek out the weak in society and give them strength and freedom to live a full abundant life through Him.

Thanksgiving Prayer

Father, I thank you for compassion on me, weak as I am. Thank you that you know everything about me, my weaknesses, my failures, my temptations. Yet you still love me. When I am weak then you are strong. Please pour your strength into my weaknesses. Help me to rely on your power and not my own. I boast in your strength, your promises, your character and not my own. Thank you that you are mine forever. In the name of Jesus, amen.

YOUR TIME

"For everything there is a season, a time for every activity under heaven." Ecclesiastes 3:1

"Yes, God has made everything beautiful for its own time. He has planted eternity in the human heart, but even so, people cannot see the whole scope of God's work from beginning to end." Ecclesiastes 3:11

"Teach us to number our days that we may present to you a heart of wisdom." Psalm 90:12 NASB

"But you must not forget this one thing, dear friends: A day is like a thousand years to the Lord, and a thousand years is like a day." 2 Peter 3:8

"Jesus Christ is the same yesterday, today and forever." Hebrews 13:8

Time is precious. We all have the 86,400 seconds each day. How are you spending yours? What are they full of? Joy? Peace? Love? Purpose? Or TV? Fighting? Stress? Anxiety? How thankful are you to have time?

How thankful are you for the seasons in your life? There is a time to study, a time to start at the bottom of the ladder and working your way up, a time to raise young children, a time to learn a new skill, a time to get through a painful situation, a time to wrestle with your God, a time to grieve and a time to smile. It may be winter, but spring is just around the corner. It may be too hot right now, but a cool wind is coming. *Nothing is permanent on earth except for the eternity that has been planted in your heart.* Time spent on connecting with the implanted eternity is not wasted.

Are you ready to ask God to help number your days? To count them out, place a purpose inside each day. If you don't number your days, what will you have to present to God in the end? What will your heart be full of? Wisdom or Waste?

Sometimes we need to step aside, stop, and think how God thinks - a day is like a thousand years and a thousand years is like a day. What does that look like? Everything that seems important right now, is not in the reality of God's thinking. This *one thing* is worth remembering. This earth-life is short. Eternity is long. What we see, is temporary. What is unseen, is forever.

One truth that is timeless - Jesus Christ is the same yesterday, today and forever. He doesn't change. His love for you doesn't change. His presence with you doesn't change. What a marvelous truth.

Thanksgiving Prayer

Oh Father, thank you for the time that you have given to me. Thank you for the years that I have lived and the years that I have left to live. Thank you that you are the one who holds my times in Your hands. I praise you for the different seasons in my life. Thank you for the season that I am in right now, a season of _____. Help me to realize fully what is permanent and temporary in my life. Please help me to number my days so that I will have a heart full of wisdom. Let me see the unseen today in my life. Thank you, Jesus, that you are the same today as you were yesterday and as you will be tomorrow. Praise you for your presence in my life. In the name of Jesus, amen.

YOUR FUTURE

"For our present troubles are small and won't last very long. Yet they produce for us a glory that vastly outweighs and will last forever! So, we don't look at the troubles we can see now; rather, we fix our gaze on things that cannot be seen. For the things we see now will soon be gone, but the things we cannot see will last forever." 2 Corinthians 4:17-18

"But we are citizens of heaven, where the Lord Jesus Christ lives. And we are eagerly waiting for him to return as our Savior. He will take our weak mortal bodies and change them into glorious bodies like his own, using the same power with which he will bring everything under his control" Philippians 3:20-21

"I focus on this one thing: Forgetting the past and looking forward to what lies ahead, I press on to reach the end of the race and receive the heavenly prize for which God, through Christ Jesus is calling us." Philippians 3:13b-14

"For I know the plans I have for you, says the Lord, they are plans for good and not for disaster, to give you a future and a hope." Jeremiah 29:11

"So, don't worry about tomorrow, for tomorrow will bring its own worries. Today's trouble is enough for today." Matthew 6:34

It's vital to cultivate an eternity mindset and focus. Take time daily to fix your mind on things that cannot be seen and thank God for them. Everything you see now on earth, won't last. Your problems, the world's troubles - they will end. It's the unseen and eternity that will be forever. Thank God for that!

Know where you truly belong. It's not here on earth or as part of a country or nation. You are a temporary resident of earth - your true citizenship is out of this world. We are new creations with new hearts and a glorious future. We are waiting for someone. Are you eagerly waiting for Jesus? The Big Change will take place when Jesus returns - weak mortal bodies will be changed into glorious bodies. What a day that will be!

Have. One. Focus. Forget the past. Look forward to the future. Press on to reach the end. There is a prize waiting in heaven - can you hear it calling?

Believe this - God's plans for you are *all* good. His plans give you a future and a hope.

Thanksgiving Prayer

Thank you, God, that my problems and the troubles of this world, people fighting people, won't last. They are only temporary. Thank you that my troubles are producing something glorious that will far outweigh any discomfort, hurt, and pain that I feel now. Thank you for the hope of your return, Jesus that there will be a day, when you will change this weak body into something glorious. Please, Father help me to have one focus here on earth- the prize waiting for me in heaven. Help me to keep moving forward in you. I praise you for the good plans that you have for me. In the name of Jesus, amen.

GOD'S PROVISION

"And this same God who takes care of me will supply all your needs from his glorious riches, which have been given to us in Christ Jesus."
Philippians 4:19

"Once I was young, and now I am old. Yet I have never seen the godly abandoned or their children begging for bread." Psalm 37:25

"You, parents - if your children ask for a loaf of bread, do you give them a stone instead? Or if they ask for a fish, do you give them a snake? Of course not! So, if you sinful people know how to give good gifts to your children, how much more will your heavenly Father give good gifts to those who ask him." Matthew 7:9-11

Here is the truth - God wants to provide for you! As His child and part of His family, He delights in providing what you need at the right time and in the right way just like a good father does. It is easy to believe that God can provide for us but it seems to be harder to believe, *does God want to provide for me personally?* Examine what you believe deep down.

Do you believe that God is able to provide in your situation? That He has *glorious riches* available to supply needs. The word *riches* in Greek is *plutos*. It means to have a fullness or abundance. He wants us to lead full and abundant lives - both here on earth and in eternity. He has a reservoir of fullness for each one of His children. A supply that never runs dry because it is in His glory. He is well able to supply fullness into your life. This doesn't necessarily mean a large full bank account but a full life. Do you believe that you can have a full abundant life without a constant full bank balance? Money is our earthly means of meeting needs but God is outside of earthly limitations, outside of time, political and economic constraints.

Do you believe that God wants to provide in your situation? If you are in Christ Jesus, then this fullness from His glory has already been given to you. It can supply all your needs. God does not abandon His own children. He is the perfect father and desires to give you good gifts.

Thanksgiving Prayer

Thank you, God, that you are a good and perfect Father who cares deeply for me. Thank you that you can provide for all my needs from your abundance and fullness in glory. Your word says that You do not abandon the godly or that Your children beg for bread. Please supply for my needs today specifically_____. God, thank for Your father heart towards me and my family. Thank you for the good gifts that You desire to bring our way. Father please help me to see Your good gifts today, open my eyes to see Your fullness, Your provision, Your care in my life. In the name of Jesus, amen.

GOD'S GRACE

"All of this is for your benefit. And as God's grace reaches more and more people, there will be great thanksgiving (gratitude), and God will receive more and more glory." 2 Corinthians 4:15, emphasis mine.

"So, God can point to us in all future ages as examples of the incredible wealth of his grace and kindness towards us as shown in all he has done for us who are united with Christ Jesus." Ephesians 2:7

"For the Lord God is our sun and shield. He gives us grace and glory. The Lord will withhold no good thing from those who do what is right." Psalm 84:11

"Christian gratitude is joy directed toward Jesus for his grace."
John Piper, desiringgod.org

Our whole purpose for living is to bring glory to God and enjoy Him forever. I never realized how intertwined these two actions are until I studied thanksgiving. When Jesus is our whole focus in life (and death), we see and experience the abundance of grace.

Grace doesn't start and end at the cross. Grace is ongoing. There is no end to the grace of God. It is limitless. It flows into every part of our lives. We receive God's favor and grace the moment that He conceived us and bought us into being inside our mother's womb. We experience the most amazing grace when say "Yes!" to Jesus and His finished work on the cross. When we open the door of our heart to God, grace floods in. Grace upon grace. We live and breathe and have our being because of His grace. We are His child and part of His family because of His grace. We have a future, a hope and destiny because of the grace of God.

"Grace" and "gratitude" come from the same original Greek root. John Piper describes this relationship when he says "When the grace of Jesus penetrates the human heart, it rebounds back to God as gratitude. Christian gratitude is grace reflected back to God in the happiness we feel toward Jesus." There is a flow happening - we receive God's abundant grace which produces a gratitude (thanksgiving) from us back to Him and He is glorified. Grace. Gratitude. Glory.

A person who is full of gratitude and thanksgiving to God because of His daily grace is happy - ecstatically happy! Yes, happy Christians bring glory to God.

"May God our Father and the Lord Jesus Christ give you grace and peace." Galatians 1:3

Thanksgiving Prayer

Thank you, Father, for your grace. Thank you for saving me, giving me a new life, a new heart, and a new future. Thank you for your son, Jesus who paid the full price for my salvation. Thank you for your love and your mercy which are new every morning. Please help me to have a heart full of gratitude. A thankful heart. A heart that has you at the center. A life bringing glory to you through giving you thanks. Thank you for your never-ending grace that flows into my life every day. I thank you that I can enjoy you and your favor on my life. In the name of Jesus, I pray, amen.

GOD'S LOVE

"But you, O Lord, are a God of compassion and mercy, slow to get angry and filled with unfailing love and faithfulness." Psalm 86:15

"You guided my conception and formed me in the womb. You clothed me with skin and flesh, and you knit my bones and sinews together. You gave me life and showed me your unfailing love. My life was preserved by your care." Job 10:10-12

"And I am convinced that nothing can ever separate us from God's love. Neither death nor life, neither angels nor demons, neither our fears for today nor our worries about tomorrow - not even the powers of hell can separate us from God's love. No power in the sky above or in the earth below - indeed, nothing in all creation will ever be able to separate us from the love of God that is revealed in Christ Jesus our Lord." Romans 8:38-39

"Perfect love expels all fear." 1 John 4:18

If we truly believe, remember and daily experience the love of God, there would be no room for fear, worries or concerns. The moment we take a worry thought and dwell on it, we have forgotten that God loves us deeply. God's very nature is compassion, mercy, and love. His love is abundant, great, strong, and enough according to Psalm 86:15. He is full of love.

It is always love first with God. Throughout the stories in the Bible there is a pattern of God loving on His people and the people turning their back on God and trying to live life without Him. He is slow to get angry. He loved us first by sending His own son to bring us back to Himself. We were in no position to love Him.

We are an expression of His love when He formed us and gave us life. When an artist or an author creates a piece of work, they put their heart and soul into the creating. Once they are finished they treat their art with care, they admire it, they share it, they maintain it and they are proud of it. It's the same with God and us. He had you as an idea then created you, gave you life, planned out your days and is preparing a place in eternity with your name on it.

Nothing, nada, under no circumstance can you be separated from God's love. It is completely impossible. Not even our worries and fears can *place room between us* (separate) and God. He is right there, with His love, always even when life gets tough and we don't feel His presence - He is still there.

Thanksgiving Prayer

Father, thank you for your compassion, mercy, and unfailing love for me. Help me to daily believe, remember and experience the width, the height and length of your love. Open my eyes to see your love in my daily moments. Thank you for the truth of your constant love - always there - never leaving or lessening. Thank you that nothing can take away that love - that it is available constantly. Give me please a heightened awareness of your love and presence right now. In the name of Jesus, amen.

GOD'S JOY

"You will show me the way of life, granting me the joy of your presence and the pleasures of living with you forever." Psalm 16:11

"The Lord is my strength and shield. I trust him with all my heart. He helps me, and my heart is filled with joy. I burst out in songs of thanksgiving." Psalm 28:7

"Those who plant in tears will harvest with shouts of joy." Psalm 126:5

"Dear brothers and sisters, when troubles of any kind come your way, consider it an opportunity for great joy. For you know that when your faith is tested, your endurance has a chance to grow. So, let it grow, for when your endurance is fully developed, you will be perfect and complete, needing nothing." James 1:2-4

There is an actual feeling of happiness, comfort, delight, and satisfaction from the presence of God. Have you felt it? If not, pray Psalm 16:11. Allow Him to show you the way of life and there you will experience His joy.

There is a place of pure contentment when we know deep down that the Lord is our strength and shield. That place where we have surrendered it all, our way of doing and being, and trust in Him fully. When we recognize that He is our true helper we are then connected to this pure joy. So much joy that it bubbles up inside of us, bursting over, that we can't contain our thankfulness.

We know that there will be dark days. Those times when we walk through the valley of the shadow of death (Psalm 23). The storms of life can buffet our boat. But we can say with the Psalmist - we shall fear no evil because the Lord's rod and staff comfort us. We may plant tears at night but in the morning, there will be shouts of joy. Believe this - your hard times right now - they are temporary, and God will use them for your good.

Therefore, we can declare, along with James, I consider this hard time as an opportunity for great joy! I consider, I recognize and see, I have studied and pondered this issue and have concluded that God is good, and He will bring good from this - this makes me joyful.

Thanksgiving Prayer

Thank you Lord for your promises. Thank you for promising to show me the way of life and for giving me the joy of your presence. Please help me to enjoy your presence and walk on your paths. I thank you for being my strength today. Thanks for surrounding me like a shield. I trust you completely. Thank you for filling my heart with joy today. Please help me to be thankful despite my circumstances.

Help me to consider my troubles as an opportunity for great joy. Give me your eyes to see what you see. Help me to endure and for my faith to come through the tests of life well. Thank you for your kindness, goodness, and your joy. In the name of Jesus, amen.

GOD'S FORGIVENESS

""Come now, let's settle this, "says the Lord. "Though your sins are like scarlet, I will make them as white as snow. Though they are red like crimson, I will make them as white as wool."" Isaiah 1:18

"He has removed our sins as far from us as the east is from the west." Psalm 103:12

"I - yes, I alone- will blot out your sins for my own sake and will never think of them again." Isaiah 43:25

"But he was pierced for our rebellion, crushed for our sins. He was beaten so we could be whole. He was whipped so we could be healed." Isaiah 53:5

"Jesus said, "Father, forgive them, for they don't know what they are doing." And the soldiers gambled for his clothes by throwing dice." Luke 23:34

"So now there is no condemnation for those who belong to Christ Jesus." Romans 8:1

"I am writing to you, little children, because your sins are forgiven for his name's sake." 1 John 2:12

One of the most significant acts in history is the forgiveness of God. The Creator of heaven and earth offered an amazing abundant life, walking with Him, and mankind rebelled. They didn't want such a close intimate relationship - they wanted to do things their own way. His love and grace are beyond our imagination, even though people continually sin, He is still willing to forgive. And when He does forgive - it's the forever kind. He removes, blots out the sin and never thinks of it again!

God's forgiveness plan involved sending His son to earth, to be one of us but not one of us. Fully human but also fully divine. Jesus took our place. Jesus took upon Himself the sins of the earth - past, present, and future. Our sins. Your sins. Your future sins are under God's flowing waterfall of forgiveness. You are no longer a slave to sin but a child of God. As His child, God no longer condemns you. What amazing news. What amazing grace.

Even on the cross Jesus took the time and effort to pray for forgiveness on the soldiers for whipping Him, piercing Him, disrespecting His name, and crucifying Him. What a Savior! It's for Jesus' name's sake that our sins are forgiven.

Thanksgiving Prayer

What a marvelous Savior you are, Lord. I don't praise you and thank you enough for the forgiveness I've found in you. Thank you for settling my sin issue. Thank you for making my sins as white as snow, for removing them as far as the east is from the west and for forgetting them. Thank you for Jesus, for His sacrifice on the cross for me. Thank you for the freedom I now have in Jesus. No condemnation because my life is now in His. Thank you, Jesus, that it's for your name's sake that my sins are forgiven. Help me to forgive others with the same forgiveness that you have given to me. In the name of Jesus, amen.

GOD'S WORD

"For the word of God is alive and powerful. It is sharper than the sharpest two-edged sword, cutting between soul and spirit, between joint and marrow. It exposes our innermost thoughts and desires."
Hebrews 4:12

"All Scripture is inspired by God and is useful to teach us what is true and to make us realize what is wrong in our lives. It corrects us when we are wrong and teaches us to do what is right." 2 Timothy 3:17

"Your word is a lamp to guide my feet and a light for my path."
Psalm 119:105

"Every word of God proves true." Proverbs 30:5

"So, faith comes from hearing, that is, hearing the Good News about Christ." Romans 10:17

"But if you remain in me and my words remain in you, you may ask for anything you want, and it will be granted!" John 15:7

A believer cannot grow spiritually without spending time in God's Word and time talking with Him. It's just like any other relationship - you need to spend time with people to get to know them. We don't read it to gain brownie points with God or make Him love us more. No, we read it to gain life. It seems so simple but why do we not take the time to immerse ourselves in the Scriptures? Maybe we don't fully understand how powerful the word is and we take it for granted.

The Bible is not just a book, or technically, a collection of books. But it's words are alive and powerful. God's words expose truth and helps us make life corrections. It is God speaking to us. Everything in it is useful for our lives. The Word shows us God's character - that He is full of love, grace, and forgiveness towards us. That He has a plan for our lives. The Bible helps us discover what our next step is - as a lamp does on a dark night.

The Bible gives us loads and loads of promises to place our faith on. The very reading of the book builds faith in our hearts. It is the ultimate life manual. It sets out eyewitness accounts of people who walked and talked with Jesus. Accounts of people and events throughout history that show us how to relate to God. The Word is a marvelous gift from God to us.

Thanksgiving Prayer

Thank you, Father, for giving us your Word, thank you that I am alive for such a time as this. I praise you for your Word, that it is living and powerful. That it is true and guides me into the right paths for my life. Thank you that when I read it, I meet with you and see your character more fully. Thank you for the faith that arises in my heart from meditating on your Word. Thank you for your wonderful promise that when your words dwell in me, when I make my requests known to you - you respond. In the name of Jesus, amen.

GOD'S CREATION

"I look up to the mountains - does my help come from there? My help comes from the Lord, who made heaven and earth!" Psalm 121:1-2

"For ever since the world was created, people have seen the earth and sky. Through everything God made, they can clearly see his invisible qualities - his eternal power and divine nature. So, they have no excuse for not knowing God." Romans 1:20

"O Lord, what a variety of things you have made! In wisdom you have made them all. The earth is full of your creatures." Psalm 104:24

God has created an amazing place for us to live, breathe, work, and play. Everything we need has been provided for in creation. Take time out and meditate on Psalm 104 - it's a full list of what God has made just for us to enjoy. The variety, the vastness, the colors, the textures, the tastes, the sounds - so many places to explore, so many animals and plants to see.

It's a spring day as I write this, the spring winds are howling outside - hailing one moment, sun streaming in the next. Bright yellow daffodils smile at me from the windowsill. Our little kitten playfully peering out from under a crumpled-up piece of paper. Green luscious grass growing at a fast pace. Seasons change but God remains the same.

The earth is filled with the glory of God. His unfailing love is everywhere. Take time today to observe the Creator in His creation.

See His provision in the sparrow carrying the worm.

See His Father heart in the mother cat licking her baby kitten.

See His cleansing forgiveness as water sweeps through the valley.

See His magnificence as you gaze at the night sky.

See His holiness as fire consumes the forest.

See His strength as you gaze at the mountains.

Hear His judgment as the clouds thunderclap.

Hear His praises as you wake to birdsong.

Hear His joy as kids laugh and giggle.

Hear His justice in the loin's roar.

Hear His heart break in the cries of the innocent.

Taste His goodness from the nectar of the bees.

Thanksgiving Prayer

Oh, thank you Father for everything that you have created for us to enjoy. From the mountains that speak of your help and protection, to the baby animals that display your nurturing heart. Thank you for your glory which is clearly shown in all of creation. Please give me eyes to see and ears to hear. Open the wisdom of your creation. Let me understand fully your message that it speaks. Thank you for creation's voice which points everyone to Jesus. Thank you Lord for the lessons in nature that you have filed away for us to discover. Praise you God, creator of heaven and earth. The Almighty One, El Shaddai. Thank you for the way you create variety and color. Thank you for your intricate design. Father, let all of creation praise your wonderful name. In the name of Jesus, amen.

JESUS' PRAYER

"Now I am departing from the world; they are staying in this world, but I am coming to you. Holy Father, you have given me your name; now protect them by the power of your name so that they will be united just as we are.

I'm not asking you to take them out of the world, but to keep them safe from the evil one.

Make them holy by your truth; teach them your word, which is truth.

I'm praying not only for these disciples but also for all who will ever believe in me through their message.

I am in them and you are in me. May they experience such perfect unity that the world will know that you sent me and that you love them as much as you love me.

Father, I want these whom you have given me to be with me where I am. Then they can see all the glory you gave me because you loved me even before the world began!" John 17:11,15,20,23-24

Take time to read Jesus' prayer for you recorded in John 17. It's amazing! Jesus is praying to the Father on the disciples and on our behalf. He says in verse 20 that He is not only praying for the disciples but for **all** believers. Ponder that, Jesus prayed for you, before you were born.

Jesus prayed for our protection so that we can be of one heart and mind together. He prayed that we would be kept safe from the enemy. He knew that it would be best if we were left in this world. There are still many, many people who need Jesus and we are His evidence of what His love can transform. Jesus doesn't want us to be left here on earth with no help. He asks the Father to teach us His word - the truth which will make us complete and set apart.

The most amazing part of Jesus' prayer is in verse 23, that the Father loves us as much as He loves Jesus. What a weighty thought. Allow that to permeate your mind. The Father loves you as much as He loves Jesus, His only begotten son.

Jesus ends His prayer asking for us to be able to see His glory. Yes, Lord we want to see Your glory!

Thanksgiving Prayer

Thank you, Jesus, for praying for me those many years ago. Thank you, Father, for the protection and safety that I find in you. I praise you for the mission that you have given to me - to be a shining light and show Jesus to everyone that I meet. Thank you for teaching me Your truth from Your Word. It's food to my soul. Thank you for the unity and love that I find in my church family because of Jesus' prayer. Thank you, Jesus, that you want me to be where you are. I want to see your glory. In the name of Jesus, amen.

JESUS' NAME

"But Peter said, "I don't have any silver or gold for you. But I'll give you what I have. In the name of Jesus Christ, the Nazarene, get up and walk!" Acts 3:6

"Therefore, God elevated him to the place of highest honor and gave him the name above all other names, that at the name of Jesus every knee should bow, in heaven and on earth and under the earth, and every tongue confess that Jesus Christ is Lord, to the glory of God the Father." Philippians 2:10

"But these are written so that you may continue to believe that Jesus is the Messiah, the Son of God, and that by believing in him you will have life by the power of his name." John 20:31

"Therefore, let us offer through Jesus a continual sacrifice of praise to God, proclaiming our allegiance to his name." Hebrews 13:15

Here is something to be very excited about - we may have very little in our bank accounts, we may be living from pay check to pay check and we may not have anything spare to give away but, we have something far more precious - the name of Jesus. That's all that Peter and John had to give the lame man begging beside the Beautiful Gate on the path into the temple. The lame man was looking for money. Peter and John gave him something that money couldn't buy - healing in the name of Jesus. This resulted in praise and thanksgiving pouring out to God for healing a lame man.

His name is above all other names - it's above cancer, it's above homelessness, it's above grief, loss, cyclones, fire, separation, sickness, pain, and death. The day is coming when everyone and everything will confess that Jesus Christ is Lord!

His name has power. This power is activated when we believe. This power creates abundant life in us. Praise God! Magnify the name of Jesus today by focusing on Him not on your problems. When Jesus is in your sight everything else pales into the background - that is magnifying the name of Jesus. Proclaim daily your allegiance to the name of Jesus by giving a continual sacrifice of praise and thanksgiving to God.

Thanksgiving Prayer

Oh, Father, I thank you for Jesus and His name. Thank you for the power that resides in His name. Thank you for the healing and life that is available in the name of Jesus. Jesus is all I need. Whatever I am facing right now - Jesus is the answer. There is power in His name to overcome everything that I will face today.

His name is above everything in my life right now - illness, financial problems, family issues, stress _____. Please help me to focus on Jesus and less on my problems today. I proclaim allegiance to the name of Jesus. I offer up a sacrifice of praise and thanksgiving to God. In the name of Jesus, amen.

OTHER BOOKS BY RACHEL LARKIN

Simple Prayer: The Guide for Ordinary People Seeking the Extraordinary

It's a call for *simple prayer*.

Are you desiring an exciting and fulfilling prayer life? – yet you feel distracted and disconnected from God?

You are not alone.

I understand the battle that you daily fight when you try to connect with God in prayer. I have discovered a simpler way to pray – a way that turns ordinary moments into extraordinary divine encounters.

Delighting in the Names of God: 8 Weeks to a Deeper Prayer Life

Delighting in the Names of God will take you on an 8-week journey of reconnecting and delighting in Yahweh through studying 7 Hebrew names of God. It's a simple way of deepening your prayer life.

This study is perfect for individuals and small groups with discussion/meditative questions at the end of each Hebrew name of God.

Find these and other helpful books at
https://www.rachellarkin.com/books/

FREE EBOOK

Life is messy. It's hard to see the spiritual in the midst of the natural. That's the challenge - to see behind the scenes of real life - to see *The Untold Story*. The story that God is weaving throughout your daily moments. *The Untold Story* eBook is an expression of a deep need in our soul to see the spiritual happening. It will not only inspire you to see the unseen, but you will also discover 7 steps to seeing God turn up in the mess of your real life.

Download your free copy from here
https://www.rachellarkin.com/book/untold-story/

ABOUT THE AUTHOR

Rachel Larkin lives in New Zealand with her husband and their three young adult sons. She writes about growing in faith and developing your potential on her website - http://rachellarkin.com/.

She is also a practicing Chartered Accountant, home-schooler for fourteen years and craves chocolate constantly.

Made in the USA
Monee, IL
15 October 2024